THE RED FEATHER

THE RED FEATHER

A Christmas Story for Every Season

A true account of the
incredible power of love and forgiveness

Tom Elliff

PUBLICATIONS
Fort Washington, PA 19034

The Red Feather
Published by CLC Publications

U.S.A.
P.O. Box 1449, Fort Washington, PA 19034

UNITED KINGDOM
CLC International (UK)
Unit 5, Glendale Avenue, Sandycroft, Flintshire, CH5 2QP

Printed in the United States of America

ISBN (hardcover): 978-1-61958-264-4
ISBN (e-book): 978-1-61958-265-1

Unless otherwise noted, Scripture quotations are taken from the New American Standard Bible® (NASB), Copyright © 1960, 1962, 1963, 1968, 1971, 1972, 1973, 1975, 1977, 1995 by The Lockman Foundation. Used by permission. www.Lockman.org

Some names and identifying details have been changed to protect the privacy of individuals.

Cover design by Mitch Bolton.

Dedicated to

Jewell Canille Carter Elliff

With gratitude
for a lifetime of
extravagant love.

Jesus was all the world to her.

Contents

Prologue

FOR OVER THIRTY YEARS I've been telling the story of the red feather, usually during the Christmas season—but not always. *The Red Feather* is a true story. I know it is true, because it happened to me, and to my family, both immediate and extended.

I also know the story of the red feather is true because it defies human imagination. While many people can identify with this story's beginning, far too few people can identify with its remarkable ending. That's why, after telling this story to multiplied thousands of people, I have decided to put it into writing.

Now, my sister and two brothers might argue a little over the minute details in the story of the red feather, and that's because each one of us has a tendency to selectively file things away in the library of our memory. But we all agree that the story is true, and that it's worth the time it will take for you to read it.

I know that some of you who are reading this have lives that seem impossibly tangled. "Is anything too difficult for the LORD?" (Gen. 18:14), God once asked

Abraham. Right now, you may feel the answer to that question is, "Yes! My problems are too difficult for anyone to solve, even the Lord." My prayer is that this little book will plant the seeds of faith and hope within your heart. You see, not even *your* problems are too difficult for God to solve. What's so amazing is that He actually delights in solving problems just like yours. I know this is so because, as the story you're about to read will prove, He has done that very thing for me!

Of all the challenges that face us, I think the most burdensome are relational, that is, how we get along with others. And of all the different kinds of relational challenges we face, I think that family problems are the most important for us to resolve successfully. But family problems can also be some of the most difficult for us to deal with effectively!

Over the years, my own family has experienced many kinds of challenges: an automobile accident that left a daughter severely injured; a house completely destroyed by fire and another dwelling destroyed by a tornado just three months later; the untimely deaths of three of our parents, each after a lingering illness; and my wife's recent battle with cancer, a battle that ended with her victorious entry into heaven, a battle I chronicled in *The Unwanted Gift*. That's just a short list! But the single greatest problem I have ever experienced was a family problem. Though it remains difficult for me to do so, I want to tell you about it.

My struggle was in the area of forgiveness. You see, no one can live an effective, joy-filled life without learning how to forgive. And those who can truly forgive are those who have themselves experienced the complete forgiveness of God. Now I know that this is true, because I have experienced that very thing myself.

What about a family problem that seems impossible to resolve satisfactorily? What if tragic decisions have already been made, and people have been deeply wounded as a result? What if those problems include serious physical illness, or even death? Can those problems have a suitable solution? They certainly can! And I can tell you how.

But I'm getting ahead of myself. I'd better start at the beginning. My story begins in a small town in southern Arkansas, during the Christmas season of 1946.

1

Christmas 1946

"THERE!" exclaimed Mother as she stood on tiptoe and stretched to place the red feather in the uppermost branches of the Christmas tree. "That's just what that tree needed, don't you think?"

My mother's eyes, green with a hint of brown, sparkled with excitement. A wide smile broke across her face as she turned, first toward my sister and then to me, her long, graceful arms folded in satisfaction. My sister, Sandy, and I stood on either side of her, gazing up at the tree. We were convinced it must surely be the most wonderful Christmas tree in the entire world.

"It's beautiful!" gasped Sandy.

"Wow, Mommy!" I added with a squeal of delight before quickly returning to play with the remnants of the decorations that were scattered across the hardwood floor.

In reality, the Christmas tree was only sparsely decorated. With the close of the Second World War, our nation was struggling to recover its economic equilibrium. Our small town traded primarily on the produce of the surrounding farms and we were especially feeling the postwar impact.

Lake Village, Arkansas clings fiercely to the willowed banks of Lake Chicot in the southeastern corner of the state and only a few miles from the Mississippi River. In a large sweeping curve resembling an oxbow, Lake Chicot follows an earlier path of the Mississippi River for over twenty miles. It was to this small town along Lake Chicot that my father brought his young family in 1944 when he assumed the pastorate of the town's First Baptist Church.

We lived in the church parsonage, a comfortable house provided by the church for its pastor and his family. The parsonage was ideally situated just down the street from the church and across the road from the lake. In addition to his family responsibilities and those associated with pastoring his church flock, my father was also the proud owner of two goats and a large blue roan horse. The goats provided much-needed milk for our family. The horse provided a recreational outlet for my dad, until it went blind—a sad fact discovered only when it was spooked by the sound of its own hoofbeats on a wooden bridge, throwing my surprised father to the ground.

Early on, our family made a tradition of decorating the Christmas tree on the weekend following the Thanksgiving holiday, a practice that remains in my own home to this day. Though not quite three years of age at the time, I still possess several vivid memories of our Christmas in 1946, including the gifts I received on that Christmas morning: a box of wooden soldiers cut out by my father on a small jigsaw, a complete set of twenty-six alphabet blocks, and a plastic ball with a face painted on it. But on that night in 1946, very few decorations ornamented the somewhat gangly spruce that had been harvested from the woods nearby and brought home that very evening by my father. The tree filled the house with a wonderful aroma I still associate with Christmas. The tree's decorations included one long strand of popcorn, carefully threaded by my five-year-old sister, Sandy, and a multicolored chain made of construction paper loops that I had glued together with the help of my mother. As a final touch, my mother methodically layered the tree's branches with store-bought tinsel "icicles."

"It still needs something," said Mother, seemingly in deep thought as we played around the sparsely decorated tree. "There's just something missing, Tommy," she said as she cocked her head toward me. "But I'm not sure what it is."

While Mother stood, hands on hips, squinting intently at the tree, our attention was drawn to the sound of an automobile as it turned from the road and into our drive. The engine sputtered to a stop. We heard the sharp ratcheting sound of the emergency brake as the driver pulled it on, followed by the squeak of an automobile door as it was first opened then firmly shut.

"I'll get it," said my father, walking toward the front door. "I can't imagine who'd be coming to see us on a cold night like this."

Situated as it was on such a large lake, the winter nights in Lake Village could seem remarkably frigid for a town so far south and so close to the Louisiana state line. This was one of those cold nights when the thick fog seemed to slip around a person's shoulders like a second coat, drawing warmth out of the body and replacing it with an icy embrace.

My father's question was answered by the unmistakable clicking of a lady's high-heeled shoes on the wooden steps leading up to our front porch. Undoubtedly, this meant we were receiving a visit from Mrs. Dr. Johnson, the wife of Dr. Johnson, our local physician. In those days, we didn't think it proper to refer to older adults by their first names. And the "Dr." in her title did not mean she was an actual medical doctor but was simply a means of distinguishing her from the other Mrs. Johnsons in the community.

Both Dr. Johnson and his wife were members of the church and noted for their gracious and generous spirits. Though just a young boy, I was captivated by Mrs. Dr. Johnson, who usually sat right in front of us on Sunday mornings. I was especially intrigued by the fox stole that was often draped over her shoulders, especially since the stole sported both the tail and the head of the fox— nose, eyes, ears and all. My mother would reach out to grab my arm as I attempted to touch the fox's nose. Putting her finger to her mouth, Mother would shake her head from side to side, signaling that I was to be quiet, sit still, and keep my hands to myself.

"You get in here and out of the cold!" insisted my father, smiling broadly as he opened the door to greet Mrs. Dr. Johnson. Mrs. Dr. Johnson was possessed of a bearing that bespoke her position in our community. She never just entered a room; she "arrived." In my young mind she was the closest thing to royalty I'd ever met. Now she was standing there in our doorway, dressed regally in a warm coat, that intriguing fox stole and the customary hat. In those days, no decent person, man or woman, would be caught dead in public without a hat, even in small towns like Lake Village. Trips to the store on Saturdays, for instance, required decent dress, and that always included a hat. Hats had a way of signaling one's position in society. Ladies, in particular, usually accumulated an array of hats to be worn on various occasions, and they stored them carefully in boxes placed high on their closet shelves. New hats, when such could be afforded, were always chosen carefully and worn proudly.

"Merry Christmas! My, what a lovely tree! Hello Sandy, Tommy, and Jewell. No, but thanks anyway, Pastor." In one breath, Mrs. Dr. Johnson simultaneously greeted each of us in the room, paid due respect to our tree, and declined the customary invitation to be seated.

"No time now," she stated matter-of-factly. "I've got a lot to do before I sleep tonight." She then held out before us an exquisitely wrapped gift box. "Here, Jewell," she smiled, referring to my mother whose name was truly suited to her personality. "This is for you. Merry Christmas!"

"For me?" Mother gasped, obviously both surprised and excited. "Whatever could it be?"

"Well, just open it and you'll find out," replied Mrs. Dr. Johnson. "I sure hope you like it. When I saw it, I said, 'That's just for Jewell.' Go ahead. Don't just stand there, open it!"

My mother sat down in a chair, placed the gift box in her lap, and began carefully removing the bow and wrapping paper, intending to save both for use later on. Opening the box, she cautiously lifted the tissue paper covering its contents inside.

"Why, it's absolutely gorgeous!" Mother exclaimed, shaking her head in amazement. "I've never seen such a beautiful hat in my life!"

"Well don't just look at it, for goodness' sake, take it out of the box," insisted Mrs. Dr. Johnson. "I think your family might like to see it, don't you?" By now, Sandy and I were at Mother's side, eager to see what the box contained.

Slowly, Mother drew the contents from the box and held it up for us all to see. She was right. It was indeed beautiful—the most beautiful hat any of us had ever seen. The hat itself was made of a dark-green felt material, with matching green netting draped across the front. But it was neither the color of the hat nor the abundance of netting that set it apart from any other we'd ever seen. What distinguished the hat was a large, bright-red feather firmly attached to one side, just above a gently curved brim.

"Oh, Mother," said my sister excitedly, "let me see it!"

"Me too!" I chimed in, actually wanting my mother to put it on my head.

"Not right now," protested my mother, turning her attention to Mrs. Dr. Johnson. "How can I ever thank you for such an absolutely beautiful gift?" Mother asked, rising from her chair and holding the hat up out of the reach of her eager children.

"It's just my way of saying Merry Christmas," replied Mrs. Dr. Johnson. "Now really, I must go. Merry Christmas to you all! By the way, Jewell, I'm really looking forward to seeing how that hat looks on you this Sunday."

With those last words, Mrs. Dr. Johnson stepped to the door, waited as my father opened it, nodded her gratitude, and departed. My father closed the door behind her, and we stood listening to the click of heels as she descended the front steps, walked to the car, started it, and drove away into the foggy night.

Oddly, when Sandy and I looked up at our mother, we were taken with the fact that she was *not* admiring her beautiful new hat. Instead, she was looking toward the Christmas tree, eyes slightly squinted and apparently in deep thought. After pensively gazing at the tree, Mother then shifted her attention to the hat in her hands.

Turning it from side to side, she ran her fingers along the edges of the red feather. With an uncharacteristic abruptness, Mother suddenly grasped the red feather, pulled it from the hat, and held it up for her surprised audience to see. Then standing on tiptoe and reaching as high as she could, Mother placed the red feather in the uppermost branches of the tree, just below the top. Before any of us could protest, Mother exclaimed, "There! That's just what that tree needed!"

My mother, in one deliberate and extravagantly generous act, had just illustrated for her family the true meaning of Christmas. In that decisive moment, she had sacrificed something of beauty and value, something that by all rights she would naturally have been expected to keep and wear proudly for others to see— and she had done it all for the benefit of those whom she loved.

That night, Mother's joyous exclamation was bound to have echoed the sentiments of the heavenly Father who, on that first Christmas long ago, might have looked down on that humble scene in Bethlehem and exclaimed, "There! That's just what this old, sin-cursed world needed—a Savior who is Christ the Lord!"

2

Christmas Through the Years

DO FEATHERS HAVE FEELINGS? I know that must sound to you like a very strange question. But I have a reason for wondering if they do.

Once that Christmas in 1946 had come and gone, the meager decorations on our tree were stored away in the twelve neat cubicles of a box that had originally contained some delicious grapefruit that friends had brought to our home. The red feather my mother had placed in the upper branches of our Christmas tree was the last thing packed away—forgotten, as most ornaments are, until the next Christmas.

By 1947, our family had moved again. We were living in Fordyce, Arkansas, a lumber mill town where my father assumed the pastorate of the First Baptist Church. After Thanksgiving, when we once again decorated our tree, we indulged ourselves with even more ornaments:

some purchased, some made at home, and some that we received as gifts from others. The tree was even more beautiful than before, adorned at the very top with an elegant angel.

In reality, there was probably not much forethought given to the act, but the last ornament placed on the tree that year was the red feather my mother had so impulsively added the year before. Dad held my sister high in the air so she could place the angel at the top of the tree. Then he held me up high as well and let me place the red feather in the limbs just below the angel. The red feather was a quiet reminder of Mother's extravagant, sacrificial love—as well as God's.

And so, with the passing of time, the final placement of the red feather became a permanent tradition when each year's Christmas tree was decorated—a rite of sorts. Our family grew with the addition of two more sons, Jim and Bill. As each child was reminded of the story behind it, he too would be held aloft by my father and allowed to place the red feather in its appropriate spot on the tree.

Do feathers have feelings? I know that's an odd question. But sometimes I like to imagine that the red feather, placed so lovingly in our family's Christmas tree on that cold winter night in 1946, had the capacity to feel what was going on around it. If so, I also imagine that each year it willingly endured eleven months of attic-bound obscurity in exchange for one month of exquisite prominence.

As the years passed, the red feather was a silent witness to the growing up, dating, courtship, and marriage of each of the four children in our family. A few years later, when my father changed pastorates once again, we moved from Fordyce, Arkansas to Kansas City, Missouri. After several years in Kansas City, Dad's ministry responsibilities brought our family back to Arkansas, where he and Mother remained until all four children had grown and left home. When each of us married and brought our new spouse home for the "first Christmas," someone would take the time to point out the red feather up in the tree, and to tell the story behind it.

With the passing of time, the red feather became more fragile and, seemingly, a bit smaller, but it was always up in the branches of the tree when we gathered for Christmas. Like a sentinel, it looked over the Christmas joys of a family that was increasing with the addition of what would ultimately be eighteen grandchildren.

Actually, I don't think feathers have feelings. But that red feather did gradually come to play a subtle but significant role in our Christmas celebrations. It was an ever-present and silent witness to the passing seasons of our family. All three of us brothers subsequently entered the ministry, and our sister married a minister. While the red feather was only mentioned around Christmas, my mother's act of selfless sacrifice, one of many on her part, was but an example of Christ's perfect love and sacrifice on our behalf.

Jesus is, indeed, just what the world needs!

3

Christmas 1981

"TOM, I CAN'T THANK YOU and the other children enough for your patience with me, and for your forgiveness."

The conversation was strained as my father and I stood in the driveway of the home where he and my mother had lived for several years. He shook my hand, looked me in the eye, and continued.

"Everything's going to be just fine. You and your family can go to Africa without worrying about anything. Trust me."

It was the day following Christmas 1981. At the age of thirty-seven, I honestly wanted to trust my father. Fathers are meant to be trusted.

Often a person's confidence in the heavenly Father is in direct proportion to the measure of trustworthiness modeled by an earthly father. But on this day my father's assurance only served to further increase the mixed emotions battling for control of my heart.

Early in 1981 God began speaking to my wife, Jeannie, and me about moving our family to Zimbabwe, Africa in order to work with national pastors and churches. This would be quite a transition for my own family that by that point included three daughters and a son. But we knew that it would mean quite an adjustment, as well, for those we would be leaving behind—particularly for my parents. I wanted to walk through the process by which we had arrived at our decision and seek their prayers and counsel. So it was with mixed emotions that I went to visit with them in their home.

In the course of our conversation that evening, my father fired a broadside at my heart.

"Since you'll be away when all this happens," he said, grimacing as he spoke through pursed lips, "I'd better just level with you about my plans."

Dad looked nervously at my mother to whom he'd been married for forty-three years, then back to me. "I have concluded that I don't love your mother anymore and I'm planning to leave."

Mother winced when Dad spoke those words, as if a dagger was being thrust into her heart. In a sense, that was exactly what was happening. Having been a pastor myself for eighteen years, I had heard others speak similar words to a heartbroken spouse, but never would I have suspected I'd hear them fall from the lips of the man who for thirty-seven years had been my hero. My father went on to explain that he was aware what he was doing was wrong. He assured me that the problem was not with my mother, but with something deep inside his own heart. Against all reason he indicated his determination to proceed with his plans.

My recollection of my father's words for the balance of that evening is lost in a blur of emotion. I don't know what such words do to a seven-year-old, but I can tell you what they do to a thirty-seven-year-old. My heart went into my shoes. I felt as if I could not breathe. My father was my champion and role model! The home in which I had grown up had been characterized by a remarkable sense of unity, peace, and security. Now, that wonderfully secure world with a united and loving family was falling apart. I could not begin to fathom the hurt and rejection my mother must have been going through as, in spite of all her best efforts, her husband had decided to walk out the door. Returning home later that evening, I told my wife the tragic news of my father's decision. We remained awake through the night, holding each other and crying out to God.

How could such a thing occur, especially in a family environment that had seemed so "right"?

Neither time nor space allows for an adequate discussion of my father's confusing plunge into a moral and spiritual abyss. Later on, however, he reflected openly about his sinful abandonment of all the principles he had known, practiced, and taught to others throughout a lifetime of ministry. He attributed his behavior to the inevitable outcome when one justs "coasts along spiritually," as he put it.

"I had forgotten the importance of daily bread," he once said with remorse. "Time with God and time in His Word is like the manna in the wilderness. It must be experienced in a fresh way every day. I allowed my heart to grow cold toward God, and in the process it grew cold toward everyone I truly loved."

"Don't make the same sinful mistake I made," I heard him say years later to a room filled with young ministers. "Any man who lets his relationship with God grow stale is open game for the devil. Not just a minister—but any man!"

When I first heard of my father's determination to leave my mother, my own family's departure for the mission field was almost a year away. We had planned to wrap things up at the church I was then pastoring, take a much-needed vacation, and then proceed to the thirteen-week missionary training conference before leaving for Africa. With overoptimistic naivety, I was confident that a little time and prayer would "fix" the problem and my prodigal father would return. Initially, it seemed as if my assumption was correct. Yes, my parent's marriage did experience wrenching, roller coaster days—days when positive enthusiasm over progress made was suddenly dashed by a temporary setback. However, my father did ultimately return home during that Christmas of 1981.

Our entire family was elated with the prospect of being together once again. We quietly rejoiced over the bright promise of a restored marriage. Grandparents and parents wrestled playfully with squirming children as family pictures were taken in front of the tree. And the red feather was a solemn witness to it all.

At the close of that wonderful day, the time for my own family's departure finally arrived. Hugs and tears abounded as we said our goodbyes, assuming it would be several years before we would return from Africa. It was a bittersweet occasion for us all. But the defining moment was my father's assurance that everything was going to be just fine. "Trust me," he had promised. Caught up as I was in the myriad details associated with our departure for Africa, I found it easier than normal to assume that the issue related to my father's wayward heart had been resolved. I was little prepared, therefore, for the news my brokenhearted mother shared with me when I called back home only a few minutes before our family boarded the plane for our overseas flight.

"He's gone, and I'm afraid this time it's for good," she said, choking back the tears. "Apparently his return home was all just an act to make your departure easier."

Suddenly, the excitement attending our journey to the mission field gave way to what I can only describe as the single most painful departure of my life.

Deep within, I knew the Lord would give my mother grace for this tragic outcome. I was assured that her many needs would be lovingly addressed by my sister, Sandy, and my two brothers, Jim and Bill, who remained near and were in constant contact with her. But that day I felt as if I was flying in the wrong direction. A few months later, when my mother received notice that my father had filed for divorce, I returned home briefly to join my sister and brothers in consoling her. I also wanted to seek out my father and make one more appeal for him to return. By that time, however, my father had moved to another state and had little desire to see me.

"You'll never guess where I found Mom the other day," my sister said as we discussed Mother's adjustment to living alone after forty-three years of marriage.

"I stopped by the house for a visit. When Mom didn't come to the door, I let myself in and began searching for her. I finally found her in the back of their closet where Dad's clothes had hung. Mom had found a coat of Dad's, and was sitting on the floor, holding his coat up to her face, rocking back and forth, and crying softly."

Dejected at the outcome of my trip, and unable to make a successful appeal to my father, I ultimately returned to Zimbabwe, to my wife and our four children. Our energies and attention were soon absorbed in the demands of adjusting to a new culture, acquiring a new language, settling our children into new schools, and making new friends. Not a day passed, however, without a painful recollection of what had happened only a few months earlier. Separated by so many miles, I could only pray for both my mother and my father.

The evening after I returned to Zimbabwe, my wife, Jeannie, and I discussed at length the tragic situation back home. I confessed to her that something new and sinister had entered my own heart. A growing sense of bitterness—a gnawing, strange and uncomfortable feeling—was invading my life. On frequent occasions,

Jeannie and I talked and prayed together about this bitterness, knowing that only God could give the grace necessary to forgive my father.

I was about to discover that God sometimes answers our prayers through a seemingly unrelated series of events, and according to His timetable, not ours.

4

Christmas 1982

"YOUR WIFE AND CHILDREN have been in a terrible accident." It was the painfully distressed voice of my friend on the other end of the line.

"Your eldest daughter has injuries that are life-threatening, and your wife is injured as well, though not as seriously. Your other two daughters and your son are fine, and they are staying with us."

I was in South Africa when I received the call, attending a training conference with a group of missionaries. Jeannie and the children had remained in Zimbabwe, with plans to drive to the northern part of the country for a retreat with missionary children. The accident occurred approximately seventy-five miles north of Bulawayo, our hometown.

The day following the accident, Jeannie and Beth, our eldest daughter, were transported by air to Harare,

Zimbabwe's capitol city, where I was waiting to meet them. Upon arriving at the hospital, our daughter was immediately taken to surgery and treated for severe burns on the right side of her body, a broken pelvis, and a broken collarbone. Jeannie was treated for a concussion and a fractured cheekbone.

Though my wife was released from the hospital on the following day, our daughter would remain for almost six weeks, allowing time for her burns and the large donor area for her skin grafts to begin healing. We settled in for the long haul, grateful that God had protected ourfamily from even more serious injuries—or worse, death.

Three days after the accident, I received a phone message from the vehicle inspection department in the town near where the accident had occurred. The officer was insisting that I come to the police station to discuss the matter.

"It was a setup." The officer's furrowed brow could not hide his own anger over the incident. I stood with him beside the crumpled vehicle as he showed me the evidence of a twisted plan gone terribly wrong.

"Actually, the ones responsible most likely just wanted your vehicle and never anticipated the tragic consequences of their selfish actions."

Later that afternoon, as I drove down the road toward Bulawayo and our home, I contemplated what the officer had said. As the road passed beneath me, I sensed the recurrence of a gnawing emotion gripping my heart. I was bitter, this time at the nameless, faceless people responsible for the accident that had left my daughter so seriously injured. Arriving home, I opened the bottom half of the Dutch door that led into our kitchen, fell to the floor, and prayed.

"God, teach me to forgive," I cried, much as I had prayed nine months earlier, not realizing in the least that He was already answering the plea of my heart.

While Beth remained in the hospital in Harare, our three youngest children returned to our home in Bulawayo, almost three hundred miles away, in order to continue their schooling. Jeannie and I traveled by plane between Harare and Bulawayo, each taking turns to insure that someone was always with Beth. In a remarkable expression of love, both Jeannie's mother and my mother traveled to Zimbabwe. Each stayed a few weeks to assist with the children before returning to the States. Jeannie and I were absolutely amazed at this sacrificial expression of love on their part, especially considering the difficulties of traveling alone. That my own mother made such a long and tedious trip to Africa still seems incredible to me. The events of the previous year had taken a severe toll on her—a fact that was immediately visible upon her arrival. But she was not to be denied the privilege of caring for her family during their own days of suffering. Our children's greatest memory of those days is of the hours she spent reading to them, creating a special bond that remained until the day of her death.

The hospital in which our daughter was being treated was also suffering severely from the loss of professional help. Zimbabwe was in the throes of surrendering control to the cruel dictatorship of a despot who often appeared to be demon possessed. The hospital staff ministered faithfully, though often apologetically, doing all they knew to do with what little equipment, personnel, and expertise remained in the country.

Five days after our friends and family back home had gathered for their Thanksgiving meal, our daughter was released from the hospital. We celebrated this milestone in her recovery with a party, joined by our missionary friends who lived in Harare and who had overwhelmed us with their loving concern. At last Jeannie and I were able to bring Beth back home to Bulawayo. We were thankful indeed for the joy of being united with our other children after so many weeks of separation.

That Christmas in 1982 was a joyous celebration for our family. Our daughter was still recovering from her injuries, a recovery that would be stretched out over many months.

But we were together again—and at home! Thus, the picture I have of our family standing before that Christmas tree in our home in Africa floods my heart with gratitude and renewed appreciation for the preciousness of life. I often thought of my mother who would be celebrating Christmas back in Oklahoma, along with my brothers, my sister, and their families. My sister helped Mother put up a small tree in the home where she lived alone. As always, the red feather was placed high among the branches of Mother's Christmas tree.

We reveled in the sunny warmth of Bulawayo, Zimbabwe during the Christmas season. The photographs, taken sometime during the holidays, include three people who had become part of our family in Africa. Ma Ndhlovu, literally "Mother Elephant," was our house helper. Her easy smile and gracious spirit made her a joy to be around.

Petros Nkala, literally "Peter the Crab," was anything but his namesake. A jovial young man in his twenties, he had literally walked out of the bush near our home, desperately seeking any kind of work in order to eat. We constructed a room for him out in our garage, and he helped with the outside work.

The third person in those photographs was another special gift to our family. Lisa Perkinson, a schoolteacher and friend, had come for an extended visit with us. Her positive, joyful spirit and eagerness to work with our children brought a sense of confidence to us all. Lisa had her own battles with lupus, a disease affecting her immune system; but she refused to be swayed by those who sought to discourage her from coming to live with us for a time. Those days in Africa became a defining moment in her brief life, a life that came to an end only a few years later. I cannot look at that photograph of our family, however, without finding myself flooded with memories that are both bitter and sweet. Our eldest daughter's smile belies the painful path she had traveled for over two months. At only fourteen years of age, she had already endured more than most adults would ever experience in a lifetime. I was still struggling with the whole matter of forgiveness. The accident—apparently a deliberate act by people who cared little for human life—coupled with my daughter's injuries, only compounded the sense of bewilderment and bitterness I was already feeling toward my father.

"Lord, teach me to forgive."

I wondered when, or even if, that prayer would ever be answered.

5

Christmas 1983

"I AGREE THAT IT WOULD BE BEST to return to the United States for the sake of your daughter."

Those words from our mission organization's regional secretary confirmed what we had already determined to be the appropriate course of action. We had visited with physicians in a neighboring country and were seriously considering how to treat the scarring that was developing, unchecked, on Beth's legs, back, and shoulder. We knew that the best help for our daughter would be available back in the States, and were encouraged by this affirmation. With the strong encouragement of our mission organization, we made preparations for our return to the United States where, not long afterward, I assumed a pastorate in Denver, Colorado.

Shortly after our move to Denver, my mother came to visit us.

"I want to see how you're set up," Mom always said to each of her children when we moved to a new location. "That way I'll have a picture in my mind when I'm praying for you."

Always bright and eager to be with her family, she'd driven to the airport in Oklahoma City, purchased her ticket, and flown to Denver. My mother was a "take charge" kind of person, not loud and assertive, but quietly pitching in wherever needed. Her trip to Africa the previous fall was a perfect example of the manner in which she approached life. "Do the hard things first," she'd said to me on more than one occasion, "and the rest will seem easy."

Mother arrived in Denver cheerful and eager to visit, but unusually tired. Over the next few days she was obviously not her normal bright and energetic self. On several occasions she seemed confused.

A simple walk around the block, for instance, resulted in a terrifying moment when Mother felt that she had become lost. We urged her to visit a physician friend of ours.

"Your mother has Alzheimer's disease," the doctor said, after calling us aside to share the news privately. His furrowed brow spoke volumes. "And based on her responses to some very simple tests, and your reports of her behavior these past few days, it is obviously advancing rather rapidly."

We were not surprised at the doctor's report. Recent articles in the newspapers about the symptoms of the disease had, perhaps, prepared us for this diagnosis. But we were perplexed and saddened that such an energetic and engaged person, a gracious woman who had already experienced her fair share of sorrow, would now be facing another sad and frightening pilgrimage.

"Life doesn't make sense," I said to my wife as we discussed Mother's situation later that evening. "She is the one who has already suffered such pain and hurt. Now, she is the victim of a frightening disease that medical science is only beginning to understand."

A few months after her initial stay with us, my brothers and their families brought my mother with them for a second visit. We celebrated Thanksgiving and put up our Christmas tree as usual on the following day. In private conversations we shared with each other just how sad it was that Dad was both physically absent and out of touch with the family.

"I wonder what Dad thinks and feels during this season of the year," I mused aloud to my wife after our extended family had returned to their homes and our house seemed unusually quiet. Because we'd talked with her about it the evening before, I knew how my mother felt. She was brokenhearted over my father's departure but remarkably conscious of the presence of God.

"I had a beautiful dream," Mother said to me that evening as we sat talking together. "In my dream I was literally nestled in the very hand of God. Ever since that time, I've really felt His peace in my heart. God will have His way with our family, and we must trust Him."

I was sure my mother was right, but I wondered if God was aware of the assignment she had given Him. I had yet to be reconciled with my father and still knew little of all that is meant by forgiving.

Mother did her best to remain focused and attentive during those few days with her family, though on several occasions she found it difficult to express herself adequately. In those moments you could see the combination of fear and frustration tracing across her normally pleasant countenance. She was not alone in her concern. Each of us realized we were entering uncharted territory.

The disease that held my mother captive advanced with surprising speed. Alzheimer's disease often impacts a person's thought processes while leaving the body relatively healthy. Sometimes, by use of proper medications, the attack on the brain can be slowed and even staved off for a significant period of time. My mother was not so fortunate. Within weeks following our Thanksgiving celebration, her usually bright and inquisitive mind began slowly slipping into the shadows of a tangled jungle, increasingly distant from the shores of reality.

Not long after our Thanksgiving celebration, it occurred to me that Mother would have difficulty decorating a tree for Christmas. Eager for any excuse to visit her, I decided to make the trip to Mother's home and help her decorate the tree. Mother seemed overjoyed and surprised to see me, even though I had called earlier to let her know I was coming for a visit. I could tell she was struggling to be at her best, but it was obvious to both Mother and me that she was laboring to remember events, especially those occurring most recently.

"Mom, we should decorate the tree," I said, walking toward the door that led to the garage. I assumed that the boxes of decorations would be found somewhere up in the attic, which was only accessible by a fold-down stairway in the garage. I was not disappointed. Peering across the poorly lit attic, I saw among the rafters the old grapefruit box, packed away with the other decorations.

Once I had brought the box, and several others like it, down from the attic, I set it on a workbench so that I could dust it off before opening it. Carefully I removed the top so that I could examine the contents. There, on top of some other ornaments and quite obviously the last item to be packed away the previous year, was the red feather.

When I reached to pick up the feather, I found that the years had taken their toll on it. It was now spindly and fragile and, like my parents marriage, it was broken in two. Lifting the feather out of the box, I began to weep as memories of wonderful Christmases past flooded my mind. Now those secure family ties, like the red feather, had been broken—and at a time when loving companionship had never been more important. I remained in the garage for a long while, determined to regain my composure so that I could encourage my addled mother.

"The last thing my mother needs is a son who is emotionally distraught," I laughed to myself as I wiped my eyes and attempted to put on my game face. I found some adhesive tape and repaired the red feather as best I could before carefully returning it to its place in the box of decorations. With the grapefruit box under one arm, I made my way back inside where Mother was waiting.

"Did you find the decorations?" Mother inquired expectantly as she turned from the tree where she had been adjusting some of the branches.

"Sure did," I replied, "and right where I thought they'd be. I need to go back up in the attic one of these days and see what else is there. I think I spotted the small wooden chest that used to hold my collection of football cards." I set the grapefruit box on the counter and carefully raised the top.

"Why, here's the red feather!" I exclaimed as if seeing it for the first time.

Holding the feather up, I looked past it and into my mother's eyes. I could tell she was about to cry and wondered how I would comfort her. At that moment, the emotions I had sought so carefully to restrain while out in the garage burst again to the surface. I was the one who was weeping. I placed the feather back in the box, rested my hands on the kitchen counter, and sought valiantly to control my sobs as my shoulders shook with grief.

Mother was immediately at my side. Turning me toward her, she placed her long, loving arms around me. I held to her like a child and listened in absolute amazement as she began to pray. For an incredibly long time my mother prayed, never uttering a confused word or an ill-spoken phrase.

My mother's prayer was one great hymn of praise and thanksgiving to God. She thanked God for her family—for each of her four children, their spouses, and their children, one by one, and she never missed a name. She thanked God for her own marriage, though now broken, and for her husband of forty-three years. Then she prayed for my father and his wife, asking God to make His way known to them. She thanked the Lord for her salvation, and for her divine sense of security during such troubling days. In prayer, Mother entrusted herself to God's care during what she openly confessed to be days of pain and perplexity. Finally, Mother prayed again for me, and for herself, that the two of us would never be reduced to wallowing in sadness, but that we would remember instead the message of enduring hope that God sent to the world that first Christmas.

"There!" said Mother, brushing my tears away and reaching for a handkerchief to do the same for herself. "Let's get that tree decorated!"

I remember little about the rest of that day spent with my mother. I know that in future days, as she became increasingly unable to express her thoughts rationally, I would simply ask her to join me in prayer. Remarkably, in prayer her reasoning and ability to communicate seemed always to improve.

That afternoo, my mother had provided me a first-hand example of what forgiveness is all about. Forgiving is a singular, deliberate decision by which you consider a person no longer indebted to you. Instead of repeatedly retrying your case against others in the courtroom of your emotions, you simply release them to God and pray that He will be as gracious with them as He has been with you. Mother could forgive others because God, through His Son, had forgiven her. By the act of forgiving, she was casting herself totally on the Lord. She had chosen to make the Lord her source of strength and joy.

With one final act, that memorable day at home with my mother came to a close. She sat in her chair as I placed the timeworn, fragile, red feather in the upper branches of her small Christmas tree. Although she was now weary and somewhat confused, deep within my heart I could almost hear Mother say, as she had so many years earlier, "There! That's just what that tree needed!"

I knew God was saying to me, "Tom, Jesus was just what this world needed over two thousand years ago. And He's what you need right now! Years ago, you trusted Him as your Savior and received His forgiveness. Now trust Him to give you the grace to forgive others—including your father."

6

Christmas 1984

"WE REALLY HAVE NO CHOICE but to move Mother from her home."

My youngest brother, Bill, was calling to tell me that the days when our mother could stay alone in her home had come to an end. It was time for her to move to a smaller place closer to his home so that she could receive the attention that her illness demanded.

Our family was on a fast learning curve as we became increasingly acquainted with Alzheimer's disease, a disease that was only then becoming widely recognized for its devastating impact. I will be forever grateful for my sister, Sandy, and youngest brother, Bill, who lived near my mother and spent countless hours each day providing for her needs. Though we had all dreaded this day, it had finally become necessary to move Mother from her home.

Mother loved her spacious and accommodating home located on a large shaded corner in a quiet neighborhood. She and my father had moved into the house fourteen years earlier, thinking of it as the ideal place in which to live out the balance of their lives. The house had Mother's touch, including the many pictures of children and grandchildren that hung on the walls of the family room.

In my mind's eye, I can still see Mother sitting there in the family room. Beside her chair was a lamp table upon which was placed her Bible, a spiral notebook, a devotional book, and her morning cup of coffee. From her chair Mother could look out into the backyard and see the raised-brick flower garden my father had constructed with such pride. But now it was time for her to move from this comfortable and familiar nest to a strange new dwelling.

Though she would soon be in need of twenty-four-hour care, we felt it would be best to do everything we could to help her maintain the sense of dignity and privacy that she treasured so much. A small duplex was found just up the street from my youngest brother's house. This would enable family members to be with Mother as often as needed. And when the time came for round-the-clock care, others could assist us in attending to Mother's needs, including many who were simply gracious and loving family friends.

With both my sister and brother nearby, it was clear that Mother would not lack for constant attention. Some of the furniture to which she was accustomed would be moved to the new location, including her chair, and the rooms would be made to look as familiar as possible. Still, we were all dreading the day she would be moved to a new home.

The day came all too soon. All four of us children were present for the occasion. We had planned for it as best we could, but it still remains one of the most agonizing days of our lives. By prior arrangement, a trusted friend took Mother for an automobile ride as we gathered in her home, deciding just how best to make the transition. We all sat solemnly around the kitchen table, a place that had held such joyous memories for us in the past. After praying, we began to seriously discuss what lay ahead.

Unknown to us, a representative from the local utility company had entered through the front door in order to shut down the utilities. He saw us at the table, listened for a few moments to our discussion, and then quietly returned to his truck after leaving us a note. "I saw that your family was having some kind of a worship service," he wrote, "and didn't want to disturb what I sensed was a special time for you. I'll come back later."

For a brief period of time following the move, it seemed that Mother's debilitating condition had been arrested. Though still somewhat confused, she was capable of caring for herself—especially with the help of other family members who tirelessly sought to meet her needs. But, in spite of all we had hoped to the contrary, Mother began again to slip deeper into the confused and fearful state so often associated with Alzheimer's disease.

In early spring, I traveled to Oklahoma in order to spend a few days with my mother. My sister, my youngest brother, and their families were living those days at the point of exhaustion, both physically and emotionally, and were needing relief, if only for a brief time. It was on that trip that I witnessed what now remains as one of my most poignant and powerful memories of my mother's love.

Mother knew exactly which food each of her family members considered his or her favorite. Through the years, whenever we had come home for a visit, she would always seek to have our favorite food prepared for the first night's dinner. Even in her confused state, Mother remembered that I loved her tuna salad (made with sweet pickles) and her banana pudding. No one could top Mom's recipe for either of those culinary delights!

Shortly after my arrival, Mother asked if I would join her in the kitchen to prepare lunch.

"I know exactly what you want for lunch," Mother said, not concealing her excitement. "Tuna salad!"

At those words, she opened a cabinet door and removed a can of tuna, saying, "You open this for me, and I'll take care of all the rest."

I took the can opener, opened the tin of tuna, drained out the water, and emptied the contents into the mixing bowl Mother had set before me.

"Now you go sit down and let me make your favorite meal," Mother insisted, guiding me to a chair at the table.

Turning back to the counter, Mother stared down at the bowl of tuna before her for what seemed an interminable period of time. She turned her head to one side and placed her hand on her chin, obviously searching the deep recesses of her mind in an attempt to remember what it was she was doing.

Before I could rescue Mother from her dilemma, she smiled and snapped her fingers as if to say, "Oh yes, I know exactly what to do." Turning toward the refrigerator, she opened its door and removed a carton of milk. Slowly, she poured the milk into the bowl of tuna, stirring it into a soggy, sickening mess.

"What's wrong with this?" Mother wailed plaintively, in almost childlike simplicity. By this time I was at her side.

"I've done something terribly wrong, haven't I?" Mother continued, her face distorted in a look of perplexity.

"Not at all," I replied, choking back my own tears and holding both of her hands in mine. "This looks great! How about letting me finish this for us?"

As she returned to sit at the table, Mother's shoulders sagged noticeably in sad resignation. I stood at the counter, looking into the confused eyes of a regal lady whose heart was filled with pain and confusion. Somehow, in a moment unknown to Mother, it was as if her ability to provide for her family had been stolen away and hidden. It would never be found again.

We sat together at the table, looking at the best I could make of the tuna after draining the milk away. Mother began picking at the flowers that were printed on the tablecloth.

"Oh, Tommy," she cried softly. "What's happening to me?"

I was at a loss to answer her question.

"I love you, Mom," I replied. "Everything's going to be all right."

Sensing Mother's rapid deterioration, our family decided to gather in Oklahoma for a combined Thanksgiving and Christmas celebration in 1984. Mother had become even more limited in her cognitive abilities, but she thoroughly enjoyed the time with the family. Once again I was impressed with just how demanding it is to care for someone with Alzheimer's disease, and how important staying in constant touch with the family becomes at such a time.

Returning to Colorado, I began to understand the struggles experienced by children who live far away from their parents during a time of need. Like my brother Jim who also lived in a distant city, I attempted to see Mother at every possible opportunity. Still, those who were close at hand bore the lion's share of the responsibility; and I have often marveled at the grace God gave them and their spouses for the huge demand placed on their lives.

Back in Denver, our church's annual Christmas celebration was of the storybook type. The crisp, cool air and abundant snow provided the kind of winter setting you see painted on greeting cards. Our children were eager to attend the candlelight and carol service, after which we'd return home to prepare for Christmas morning.

With our church family, we joined together excitedly for the candlelight and carol service. That night I spoke briefly to the congregation about the amazing love of God, a love so powerful that it moved Him to provide His own Son as a sacrifice for our sin. I spoke of the opportunity God was providing each of us: the opportunity to spend our eternity with Him.

Seeking a way to illustrate the powerful, motivating force of God's love, I called to mind that Christmas in Lake Village, Arkansas so many years before, and my mother's impulsive, extravagant act as she took the red feather from a beautiful hat and placed it on the tree for our family to enjoy. Holding back my emotions, I told the story of the red feather for the very first time.

Rising on Christmas morning, long before anyone in our house had awakened, I went in to build a large fire in the fireplace of our family room.

I wanted everything to be just right for our family's traditional Christmas morning exchange of gifts. I knew that in another hour or so when the children arose, the same quiet family room would be the scene of joyous bedlam.

With a cup of coffee in hand, I sat by the fire for a few quiet moments. I began to meditate on all that had happened over the past several months. My thoughts turned toward my mother, and I wondered what her Christmas celebration would be like that morning. Looking at our tree, I recalled that my sister had decorated a small tree in Mom's new home.

"Yes," she had told me when I asked, "the red feather is there in Mother's Christmas tree."

My thoughts were interrupted by the sound of gentle knocking at our front door. At first I thought I must have been mistaken, but then I heard it again. Rising from my chair, I went to the door, wondering who would be out this early on Christmas morning.

A scene of stunning serenity greeted my eyes when I opened the door. Stars in abundance filled the cloudless sky and a smooth blanket of snow lay across the lawn. The air was perfectly still as I stood gazing at the scene before me. It was a perfect Christmas morning in Colorado, and it almost took my breath away.

Looking down, I noticed fresh footprints across the otherwise unblemished blanket of snow, footprints that led to the front porch, then back again toward the street. I turned, half expecting to meet someone, but saw instead only a cardboard box placed on the porch beside our front door.

"What could this be?" My words filled the air with an icy vapor as I spoke aloud to no one but myself.

Reaching down, I prepared to lift what I thought would be a heavy box. To my surprise the box was apparently empty. "This is as light as a feather," I remember thinking to myself. Turning toward the street again, I peered into the predawn darkness attempting to locate the person who had delivered the box. The bearer of the box had disappeared. I brought the box out of the cold and into the warmth of our family room. Placing it on the floor before my chair, I cautiously began to open it, concluding that it was probably an empty container that had been blown about by an earlier wind, finally coming to rest on our porch. Once the box was opened, I figured that my assumption was correct. "Left over from our neighbor's party the night before," I thought out loud.

But as I began to close that box, my eyes caught sight of something down in the dark shadows of a corner. Carefully, I removed a handwritten note with a red feather attached.

A friend of mine who had been present at our church's candlelight and carol service the night before had penned the note. As best I can recall it now, it read, "Your mother's story touched my heart, especially the part about the red feather. Now you will have a red feather in your family's tree as well. I pray it will serve as a constant reminder to you of your mother's extravagant love—and of God's as well. Merry Christmas."

I sat in the quietness of the room, interrupted only by the crackling fire, and thanked God for my mother and for her extravagant, impulsive love. And I thanked God for His love as well—a love that made it possible for my mother, and for each of us, to experience His forgiveness of sin and to spend our eternity with Him.

That morning, after our family had opened all the gifts and as we prepared for breakfast, I had an announcement to make.

"There's something up in the tree this morning that wasn't there when we went to bed last night," I said. "I wonder who can find it."

It wasn't long before the red feather was located by one of the children, and I had the privilege of telling them of my friend's impulsive, thoughtful gift that Christmas morning.

Back in Oklahoma, my sister and her family, along with my youngest brother and his family, spent their Christmas day with Mother. One subject dominated the conversation as we talked by phone that evening. It appeared that, as much as we personally dreaded the thought of it, our mother was preparing for her final journey home.

7

The Journey Home

"MOM, LET'S GO FOR A DRIVE, just the two of us," my brother would often say to my mother, knowing the drive would be a pleasant diversion from her otherwise homebound life.

"Where would you like to go?" he asked once they were seated in the car for one of these rides.

"I want to go home," Mother insisted with a sense of urgency.

Mother came from a large family, not an unusual occurrence in the early 1900s, and was reared by godly parents on a farm in South Central Arkansas. In spite of the fact that a set of twins died shortly after their birth and another brother died of complications related to his asthma, there were still eleven children in the family. Mother was the youngest in the family, and was often teased about the special treatment she got from her father, who was a county judge as well as a farmer. Until her father's death at the age of ninety-seven, the annual reunions for Mother's family were always held on Christmas Day, down at what was fondly referred to as the "home place." The home place, located out in the country and nine miles from the nearest town, was especially suited for family reunions.

A large porch, positioned like embracing arms on two adjacent sides, wrapped around the front of the house. An additional "eating porch," where lunch and dinner were served in the summer months, was located at the rear of the house, complete with a water well that never failed to produce cool, pure water. Beyond the back porch and near the fence lay the smoke house, an egg house, and a vegetable garden. Close by were the wood-shed, hen house, and potato shed. Further down the lane one could find the blacksmith shop, wagon barn, mule barn, hog lot, and cow barn. An apple orchard was located across the road, and the vegetable garden was graced by a large arbor on which grew "scuppernongs," a hardy, thick-skinned type of grape popular in that part of the country.

For several years after my grandfather passed away, family reunions were still held annually at the home place, but on Memorial Day weekends instead of Christmas

Day. Even though Mother's Alzheimer's disease was taking its toll, Mother longed to attend the family reunion on Memorial Day 1985.

"I want to go home."

At first, my youngest brother, Bill, had thought Mother was speaking of her heavenly home. But after repeated discussions, she had made it clear that she was speaking of going to the "home place." Bill determined to take Mother to the reunion, in spite of the difficulties they might encounter.

The trip to the home place included both a plane ride and a drive of almost three hours—arduous for anyone, but especially someone in Mother's fragile health. Mother, however, seemed to grow with excitement the closer they came to her home place.

At last, Bill turned the car off the asphalt road and onto the unpaved country road, down which they'd find the home in which Mother had been reared. Slowly, they drove past the leaning remnants of an old cane mill, then around a bend where the community blacksmith shop once stood, turning at last down the lane that would take them to the home Mother longed to see.

"There's that home I love so much!" Mother exclaimed, clapping her hands with gleeful excitement as the farmhouse came into view.

From the moment Mother saw the old home place, a remarkable transformation took place in her personality. It was as if the fog of Alzheimer's disease had temporarily lifted. Throughout those three days with her family, she was amazingly engaged and responsive. Mother thoroughly enjoyed every minute with her family, finally succumbing to exhaustion only as they began on the return trip home. Those days are a testimony to the power and strength one can draw from a loving family.

"Your mother is under a full-bore attack," a close personal friend once commented as I described to him the mental, and now physical, deterioration that we were witnessing on a daily basis. Alzheimer's disease was now taking ground in an unrelenting fashion.

My sister and youngest brother kept the family updated on the struggles Mother was having. Reflections of herself in mirrors or windows generated fears that another person was in the house. Tending to her personal needs became an impossible chore for this lady who had always been meticulously groomed and neatly dressed. Her own children were now periodically viewed as strangers. The look in Mother's eyes revealed painful attempts to bring order to the thoughts that had become terribly twisted in a mind that was once considered one of the brightest around.

Occasionally, Mother would seem herself for a few moments, recalling entire hymns or lengthy passages of poetry. Not surprisingly, it was still when praying that Mother seemed quite healthy and normal. In a remarkable fashion, you could literally converse with her, if your conversation was conducted "as unto the Lord." Much sooner than we imagined, Mother would, in fact, meet her Lord.

"Mom has suffered a massive brain hemorrhage. She probably has only hours to live."

The urgent call from my youngest brother, Bill, was totally unexpected. We had assumed that, like many Alzheimer's disease patients, our mother would gradually become physically debilitated, then totally bedridden; and we had discussed what we would do when that time came.

None of us, however, were prepared for my brother's news. Later that evening I was at Mother's hospital bedside along with Bill and my sister, Sandy. Our brother Jim was in Romania at the time. We could not reach him for several days, but he came immediately once he received the news.

"It will probably be only a matter of hours," said Mother's doctor, confirming the news my brother had shared with us. "She has a few days at the most. But I can tell you that essentially your mother is gone. We will keep her comfortable here, making sure she has plenty of oxygen and fluids, but the hemorrhage is quite large and it appears that her death is imminent."

While saddened, of course, by the news of Mother's impending death, each of us also admitted to a certain sense of relief. It had been a long, tedious journey from that day she was originally diagnosed with Alzheimer's disease, a journey not without its special moments of shared love and joy, but a difficult journey nonetheless. Knowing the promises of God, we were confident that "to be absent from the body is to be present with the Lord" (see 2 Cor. 5:8). We were ready to give her up to God. We were comforted with the assurance that soon all the pain and struggles associated with her life on this earth would be cast off, and Mother would be in the arms of Christ her Savior.

Standing at Mothers bedside, we cried, prayed, sang, and wept, hoping somehow to convey to our mother that we were each releasing her to God. We assured our comatose Mom that, like the apostle Paul, she had fought the fight, kept the faith, and finished the course; now she could die knowing that there was laid up for her a "crown of righteousness, which the Lord, the righteous Judge, [would] award to [her] on that day"(2 Tim. 4:8).

But God had more for our mother to do before her departure! She didn't die within a few hours! In fact, it wasn't until almost five weeks later that Mother passed away. In some miraculous, unseen way, she just "dug in."

For the next several days Mother lay comatose, making no movement and offering no communication. It seemed as if her frail body was growing smaller before our eyes, and that death should surely come at any moment. Yet Mother remained alive.

"Want! Want! Want!" Those words, falling urgently from my mother's lips, stirred those at her bedside into action.

"What is it Mother? What do you want?"

There was no response.

"Do you want water? Your pillow fluffed? Ice?"

Still no response.

"Is there someone you want?" The names of friends and family were called out, but my mother remained unresponsive.

"Is it Dad?" someone asked, expecting that there would still be no response. But at the mention of my father, my mother stirred once again and uttered a word that she actually repeated three times that day.

"Forgive! Forgive! Forgive!"

Then, again she lapsed into a coma.

The following morning, we gathered around Mother's bed, planning for the events of the day. We were startled by the ring of the phone near her bed. I reached for the phone, fully imagining that it would be a call from some friend of the family who, like so many, would be calling to assure us of prayer. The voice on the other end caused my heart to leap with excitement.

It was the voice of my father.

"I understand your mother is ill." You could hear the trepidation and uncertainty in my father's voice.

"Dad, she's more than ill," I responded. "She's about to die."

"Could I speak with her?" my father continued. I could tell that his voice was quavering and could only imagine the courage it took for him to call.

"Mom is in a coma," I replied, "but I'll place the phone beside her ear and you can tell her what you'd like."

I have no idea what my father said to my mother, but the next few minutes were a testimony to the amazing, restorative power of reconciliation. Mother's eyes opened slightly, and tears began flowing down her cheeks.

"Of course I forgive you," she said, barely speaking above a whisper, but with understanding and clarity of thought.

Over the next twenty-four hours, Mother verbally communicated her love and concern for those around her. She was especially concerned that others would experience the forgiveness of God.

"I've got to tell more people about Jesus," Mother said, as she drifted in and out of her comatose state.

For the next several days, our father would often call to inquire about Mother's condition. During one of those calls, he asked if perhaps Mother was waiting for something to happen before passing away.

"I don't know, Dad," I responded. "Maybe she's waiting on you."

"I'll be there in the morning," Dad replied immediately. "Can someone meet me up at the airport?"

It would be difficult to describe all that took place as our family was joyfully reunited the next morning. We were together again for the first time in over three years—each of the four children, three of our spouses, our mother, and our father, who was now her forgiven former husband.

"I'd like to be alone with Jewell," said my father, encouraging all of us to leave the room. Though the words spoken behind the closed door were indistinguishable, the sobs were not. Dad remained there with Mother a long time before inviting us back in the room.

Throughout the afternoon, we all remained at my mother's bedside. We cried, prayed, and even sang as Mother laid comatose, perfectly still and barely breathing. I thought of how it was my mother's forgiving spirit that had made this moment possible, and remembered the words of Edwin Markham's poem "Outwitted."

> *He drew a circle that shut me out—*
> *Heretic, rebel, a thing to flout.*
> *But Love and I had the wit to win:*
> *We drew a circle that took him in!*

There, on her deathbed, Mother had brought her family together with a spirit of love and forgiveness.

A few weeks after that remarkable reunion at Mother's bedside, a surprisingly large crowd gathered in the bright sunlight of an early fall afternoon. They had come to the small country cemetery to pay their last respects to my mother. Her freshly dug grave was located among those of many other family members who, over several generations, had been buried in that idyllic setting.

As each of Mother's children took one final look at the casket, we cherished our own thoughts regarding the person whose earthly remains were inside it. We recalled her winsome smile and quick wit, her beautiful hands, and those long, loving arms that seemed able to wrap totally around you. But mostly we recalled that our mother, bruised by a sad separation and stricken as she was with Alzheimer's disease did not go down in defeat, but in glorious triumph. In some ways, Mother's last days were perhaps her greatest days. They were days in which, often unconsciously, Mother reinforced all she had taught through the years about loving—and forgiving.

On the marble headstone at Mother's grave are chiseled these words from her favorite hymn, words that reveal the source of her loving and forgiving spirit, "Jesus is all the world to me."

Epilogue

"**WHERE ARE WE GOING?**" my father asked a few years ago when I promised him the trip of a lifetime as a Christmas gift.

"Oh," I responded, "it's not simply the trip of *a* lifetime. It's the trip of *your* lifetime."

I explained to my father that all four of his children were going to take an automobile trip with him, retracing the steps of his life. My father, then eighty-nine years of age, was skeptical (I don't blame him!), but a few months later we pulled it off. It was a thoroughly enjoyable experience, and over a three-day period we captured ten hours of video history to prove it!

At the end of one very long day, we found ourselves not far from where Mother is buried.

"We need to go by Jewell's grave," my father said. "I've never been there, and I want to see it."

Somberly, and with mixed emotions, we turned the automobile off the main highway near Warren, Arkansas and made our way down a country road to the Moseley Cemetery, where so many of my forebears are buried. Walking past the headstones was like taking a trip through history. Upon seeing some of the names, I could recall stories I'd heard as a child—stories that revealed the character of the person whose remains now lay below the ground.

When we came to my mother's grave, we noticed that sometime earlier someone unknown to us had placed flowers there. We could not help weeping, and my father wept most of all. At first, the grief of his earlier decision consumed him, but soon that gave way to tears of joy in the knowledge that he was forgiven—forgiven by his former wife, forgiven by each of his children, and most importantly, forgiven by his heavenly Father.

I've said this book contains a story of enduring love and forgiveness; and in a sense, I know it's much more than that. It is a simple tribute to my mother, and an expression of heartfelt gratitude to the one who taught me the wonderfully liberating principle of forgiveness.

Forgiveness is not the same thing as reconciliation, restitution, or approval of sin. Forgiving, according to Jesus in his parable of the unforgiving servant (see Matt. 18:21–35), involves a singular decision of the will by which you consider another person no longer indebted to you.

In that same parable, Jesus draws attention to the fact that an unforgiving person lives with a desire for retribution. That desire becomes like an acid that eats a container from the inside out. An unforgiving person cannot live a life of faith because he believes someone other than God holds the key to his joy. An unforgiving person, therefore, lives a life of sin and is unpleasing to God. He is in a prison of uselessness and out of fellowship with the heavenly Father. He has made his own heart into a dungeon in which he has imprisoned those he won't forgive, and he lives in personal torment as a result.

How liberating it is to practice forgiveness! And believers in Christ, those who have repented of sin and trusted in Him alone for salvation, can forgive others because they themselves are forgiven. The story of Jesus is called the gospel, or "good news." In that story we discover that because of Christ's life, death, and resurrection, we can come to God, receiving both forgiveness and eternal life. That's good news for us, as well as for others. Having been forgiven ourselves, we can now forgive those who in any way have offended us.

Shortly after my mother's death, all four of Mother's children gathered once again to disperse what little remained of her earthly belongings. Unlike some estate settlements that I've heard about, this one was an experience in which the statement, "No, you take that because Mother would have wanted you to have it!" was heard again and again. Finally, we decided just to put numbers on everything, draw straws, and force everyone to pick something when their time came.

I became amused noticing that some of us had our eye on the old grapefruit box in which were placed the Christmas decorations, including the red feather. I don't remember who got the box. But I do remember the gasp of surprise when it was excitedly opened and the red feather was missing! It was almost as if Mother, with that twinkle in her eye and wry smile, was saying what my friend had said earlier, "It's time for you to get your own example of God's extravagant love."

I've shared this true story with a prayer. I pray that you will choose to be both *forgiven by God* and *forgiving of others!*

As my friend wrote on that Christmas day, "It's time for you to get your own red feather."

PUBLICATIONS

Fort Washington, PA 19034

This book is published by CLC Publications, an outreach of CLC Ministries International. The purpose of CLC is to make evangelical Christian literature available to all nations so that people may come to faith and maturity in the Lord Jesus Christ. We hope this book has been life changing and has enriched your walk with God through the work of the Holy Spirit. If you would like to know more about CLC, we invite you to visit our website:
www.clcusa.org

To know more about the remarkable story of the founding of CLC International we encourage you to read:

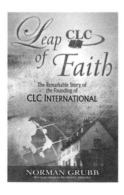

LEAP OF FAITH

Norman Grubb
Paperback
Size 5¼ x 8, Pages 248
ISBN: 978-0-87508-650-7
ISBN (*e-book*): 978-1-61958-055-8

THE BROKEN CURSE

Tom Elliff

A cruel remark or a biting criticism can become like a curse. It has the power to set the course of your life. But, in Christ, there is freedom from that curse. Tom Elliff knows this from personal experience. In *The Broken Curse*, he shares his story of personal deliverance, along with God's "secret" for breaking the curse of words.

Hardback
Size 5 x 7, Pages 87
ISBN: 978-1-61958-241-5
ISBN (*e-book*): 978-1-61958-242-2

THE UNWANTED GIFT

Tom Elliff

In this book, Tom Elliff shares how he and his late wife, Jeannie, came to view their toughest challenge as a gift. Through biblical study and reflection on a personal trial, he demonstrates how to accept that hardships bring life's greatest measure of God's grace and power. Our most painful problems, though unwanted, can truly be gifts from God.

Hardback
Size 5 x 7, Pages 102
ISBN: 978-1-61958-234-7
ISBN (*e-book*): 978-1-61958-235-4

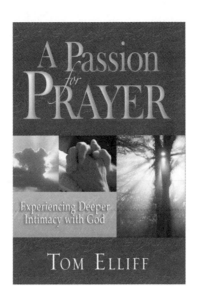

A PASSION FOR PRAYER

Tom Elliff

Of all the disciplines of the Christian life, prayer is perhaps the most neglected. Yet Jesus' brief earthly life was permeated with it. *A Passion for Prayer* seeks to help you develop—or deepen—your communion with God. Drawing on personal experience and God's Word, Pastor Tom Elliff shares principles for daily coming before the throne of grace.

Paperback
Size 5¹/₄ x 8, Pages 252
ISBN: 978-1-936143-03-0
ISBN (*e-book*): 978-1-936143-26-9

THE PATHWAY TO GOD'S PRESENCE

Tom Elliff

The Pathway to God's Presence encourages those who feel they have lost the sense of God's presence in their lives and wish for restoration. Examining the Old Testament account of Moses and the children of Israel, the book highlights the distinction between "God's provision and His presence."

Paperback
Size 4¹/₄ x 7, Pages 140
ISBN (*mass market*): 978-1-61958-156-2
ISBN (*trade paper*): 978-1-61958-170-8
ISBN (*e-book*): 978-1-61958-157-9

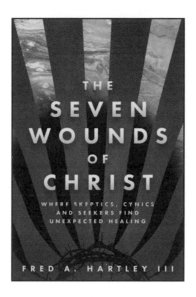

THE SEVEN WOUNDS OF CHRIST

Fred A. Hartley III

In *The Seven Wounds of Christ*, Fred Hartley shares how Christ's wounds on the cross represent the fullness of His atonement and how, individually, each wound corresponds to a distinct healing for us. Using straightforward scientific explanations, real-life stories and biblical truths, Hartley teaches that no matter the depth of our wounds, the wounds of Jesus go deeper—and His wounds are for our healing.

Hardback
Size 5 x 7, Pages 151
ISBN: 978-1-61958-258-3
ISBN (*e-book*): 978-1-61958-259-0

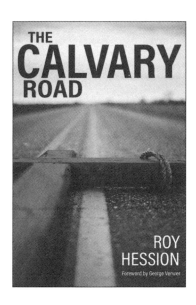

THE CALVARY ROAD

Roy Hession

Do you long for revival and power in your life? Learn how Jesus can fill you with His spirit through brokenness, repentance and confession in this updated version of Hession's classic, *The Calvary Road*. In the course of eleven chapters, Hession emphasizes the need for personal revival in life with Christ.

Paperback
Size 4^1/$_4$ x 7, Pages 162
ISBN: 978-1-61958-226-2
ISBN (*e-book*): 978-1-61958-227-9

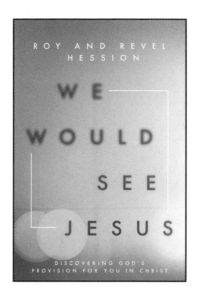

WE WOULD SEE JESUS

Roy and Revel Hession

In this classic companion to the best-selling book *The Calvary Road*, Roy and Revel Hession teach that seeing Jesus is the answer to every aspect of our Christian life. Painting a refreshing and challenging picture of the Lord Jesus, they tell of Him in whom all the needs of human hearts are met. Two themes occur again and again in these pages—grace and revival—but the main direction and theme is always Jesus.

Paperback
Size 4^1/$_4$ x 7, Pages 189
ISBN: 978-1-61958-266-8
ISBN (*e-book*): 978-1-61958-267-5